SHORT • SCENIC • WALKS

THREE PEAKS
& MAL...

PAUL HANNON

HILLSIDE PUBLICATIONS
2 New School Lane, Cullingworth, Bradford BD13 5DA

First Published 2021 © Paul Hannon 2021

ISBN 978 1 907626 33 3

While the author has walked and researched all these routes for the purposes of this guide, no responsibility can be accepted for any unforeseen circumstances encountered whilst following them

Sketch maps based on OS 1947 1-inch maps

Cover illustrations: Stainforth Force; Malham Cove
Back cover: Upper Ribblesdale; Page 1: Above Crummack Dale
(Paul Hannon/Yorkshire Photo Library)

Printed in China on behalf of Latitude Press

HILLSIDE GUIDES... cover much of Northern England

- 50 Yorkshire Walks For All
- Journey of the Wharfe (photobook)

Short Scenic Walks
- Three Peaks & Malham
- Wharfedale & Ilkley
- Ribble Valley & Bowland
- North York Moors
- Teesdale & Weardale
- Harrogate & Nidderdale
- Wensleydale & Swaledale
- Ambleside & South Lakeland
- Arnside & Lunesdale
- Aire Valley
- Haworth
- Hebden Bridge
- Around Pendle

Walking in Yorkshire
- North York Moors South & West
- Nidderdale & Ripon
- Wharfedale & Malham
- Aire Valley & Bronte Country
- Yorkshire Wolds
- South Yorkshire
- Three Peaks & Howgill Fells
- North York Moors North & East
- Wensleydale & Swaledale
- Harrogate & Ilkley
- Howardian Hills & Vale of York
- Calderdale & South Pennines
- West Yorkshire Countryside

Lancashire/Cumbria/North Pennines
- Pendle & the Ribble
- Eden Valley

Visit us at www.hillsidepublications.co.uk

CONTENTS

Introduction 4

1 Mastiles Lane 6
2 Malham Tarn 8
3 Malham Cove 10
4 Gordale Scar 12
5 Around Pikedaw Hill 14
6 Aire Head Springs 16
7 Kirkby Malham 18
8 River Aire 20
9 Langber Lane 22
10 Cleatop Park 24
11 The Settle Hills 26
12 Around Langcliffe 28
13 Giggleswick Scar 30
14 Stainforth Force 32
15 Catrigg Force 34
16 Smearsett Scar 36
17 Feizor's Woods 38
18 Crummack Dale 40
19 Long Lane 42
20 Sulber Nick 44
21 Around Horton 46
22 Hull Pot 48
23 Thorns Gill 50
24 Ribblehead Viaduct 52
25 Chapel-le-Dale 54
26 Kingsdale 56
27 Waterfalls Walk 58
28 Newby Moss 60
29 Norber Boulders 62
30 Trow Gill 64

Clapham

Janet's Foss

INTRODUCTION

Whilst the south-western Yorkshire Dales may be dominated by the celebrated trio of Whernside, Ingleborough and Penyghent, the landscape of Three Peaks country and Malham holds a much greater appeal in its remarkable limestone formations. This natural wonderland boasts an astounding array of gleaming scars and pavements, an unparalleled assembly of gaping potholes and labyrinthine caves, deep ravines, sparkling waterfalls, and also a network of inviting green trackways over the hills.

The buzzing little town of Settle makes a perfect base, and is supported by a delectable range of villages such as Stainforth and Langcliffe, Horton and Austwick, Clapham and Ingleton. Focal point of the region is the River Ribble, and all around are absorbing landmarks from Smearsett Scar and the Norber Boulders to Stainforth Force and Warrendale Knotts. The Settle-Carlisle Railway runs through the very heart of the district, dominated by the iconic Ribblehead Viaduct. Giving birth to the River Aire, adjacent Malhamdale takes its name from the village for which all visitors make. Although its river has but a brief existence in these tranquil pastures its time is well spent, and presents a highly compact area that offers some simply incomparable limestone scenery based on Malham Cove, Gordale Scar and Malham Tarn.

The majority of walks are on rights of way or established access areas and paths: a handful which cross Open Access land are noted as such. Most days of the year you can freely walk here, but dogs are banned from grouse moors other than on rights of way. These areas can occasionally be closed, most likely from the grouse-shooting season's August start, though weekends should largely be unaffected: details from Natural England and information centres. Whilst the route description should be sufficient to guide you around, a map is recommended for greater information and interest: Ordnance Survey Explorer maps OL2 and OL41 cover the walks.

- Yorkshire Dales National Park, Bainbridge, Leyburn DL8 3EL (0300-456 0030)
- National Park Centre **Malham** BD23 4DA (01729-833200)
- Tourist Information, Town Hall **Settle** BD24 9EJ (01729-825192)
- Tourist Information, Community Centre Car Park, **Ingleton** LA6 3HX (015242-41049)

THREE PEAKS & MALHAM 30 Short Scenic Walks

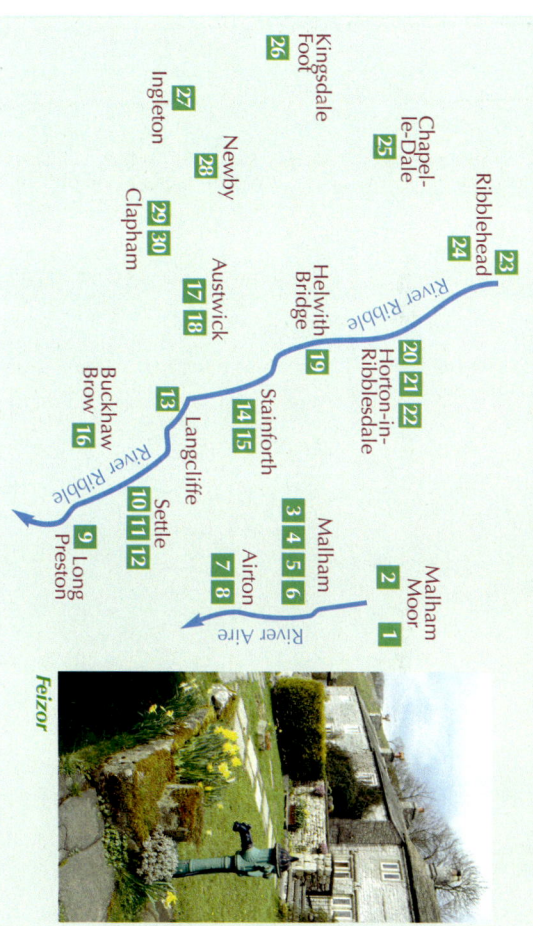

Feizor

1   MASTILES LANE

4½ miles from Malham Moor

Easy walking on a famous old way and a variety of upland paths

Start *Street Gate (SD 904656; BD24 9PR), roadside parking at minor junction half-mile east of Water Sinks Gate car park, two miles above Malham*
Map *OS Explorer OL2, Yorkshire Dales South/West*

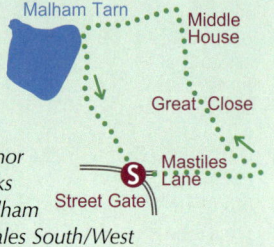

Where the road turns south at this crossroads, go straight ahead on a branch that quickly loses its surface at Street Gate. Ignoring the access road left, pass through the gate and head away on the quickly improving wallside track of Mastiles Lane. Best known of the Dales' old roads, this classic route was used by the monks of Fountains Abbey to cross from Kilnsey in Wharfedale to their sheep pastures in the Malham area. The way drops to the upper reaches of Gordale Beck, crossed by ford and clapper bridge. Passing through a gate to climb up the other side, easily missed are the faint outlines of a Roman marching camp. It probably dates from the second half of the 1st century, when the invaders were attempting to subdue the local Brigantes, a major Iron Age people of the district. As the going eases an information panel occupies a boulder to your left alongside an ancient cross base. Rising gently a little further towards a brow, just over to the left your next path can be seen doubling back across the slope. The brow proves to be the turning point, where low walls surround a water tank.

Doubling sharply back, the initially faint path gradually swings away from the track, dropping past a reed-fringed pool. The path curves right and crosses a streamlet, then over a gentle brow. Down to your left is the infant Gordale Beck, while your target of Middle House Farm is some distance ahead. After a briefly fainter spell undulating across the grassy swathes of High Stony Bank, the clearer continuation slants left down towards a wall corner: before reaching it bear right to contour the short way across to find a wall hidden in a dip. Cross the stile and continue away, crossing a green track to resume as a clear grassy track across another vast pasture, Great Close. Ahead is Middle House Farm, and at the end you converge with a wall from the left to take a stile/gate in it. Cross to a gate by an outer wall corner just ahead, then advance with the wall until it angles slightly more towards the farm. Here bear left to cross the farm road to a stile just above.

Turn sharp left (not quite as per map) on a soft grass track across the pasture of West Great Close to a stile by the left-hand of two gates at the end. Ignoring a tractor track rising left, a nice path winds up with a fence to the brow between Great Close Hill and Highfolds, revealing a magnificent prospect of Malham Tarn. The path then drops down to join the access road along the tarn's shore (see also Walk 2). Turn left on this, with the tarn on one side and the sheer limestone cliff of Great Close Scar on the other. The track runs out past the tarn to a gate onto the open moor. Remain on this firm driveway as it rises past a small wood and crosses the grassy moor to emerge onto the road exactly at the start.

At Malham Tarn

2 — MALHAM TARN

4¼ miles from Malham Moor

Almost entirely level walking on spacious limestone uplands

Start Water Sinks Gate (SD 894658; BD24 9PR), car park on Malham Tarn road 2½ miles above Malham
Map OS Explorer OL2, Yorkshire Dales South/West

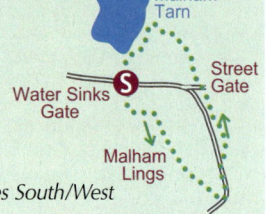

From the car park cross the road and go briefly left to head south on a path slanting gently left up to a ladder-stile in a wall ahead: look back to see the tarn beneath Fountains Fell. Across, the path enters Prior Rakes, an extensive sheep pasture recalling the wealthy landowning interests of Fountains Abbey. The path runs quickly on to another path junction alongside some pools. These are dewponds, created in monastic times to help slake the thirsts of cattle in these dry limestone uplands. After the first pool bear left on a thinner path rising gently away, with a wall over to the left. Keep right at an early fork to rise very gently alongside a low line of rocks entirely on your right, becoming the more expansive pavements of Broad Scars.

As the one and only low outcrop on your left is reached on the brow, big new views look south and east beyond some nearer limestone pavements. The path veers left past it and down through low scars to merge with a broader green path. Bear right on this across Malham Lings to a stile/gate onto a road just above the start of its steep drop towards Malham. Retain height by doubling back left, the road quickly opening out with a broad verge. At a gate on the right after some sheep pens, make use of Open Access by entering a vast pasture: a broad, grassy way bears left, and curves along midway between the wall to your left and low limestone scars to your right. Angling slightly nearer the wall, at a fork either branch will do as both merge with a broad, grassy path coming along from upper Gordale. Bear left on this, closing in on the wall and ignoring a stile to continue to the very end. Here a stile in a moist corner admits onto the historic crossroads of Street Gate.

Here the celebrated Mastiles Lane heads off right (see Walk 1). Pass neither through the gate nor left to the moor road, instead bear right along a stony, wallside road. This runs to a cattle-grid alongside tiny Great Close Plantation. Immediately across, take a more inviting grassy way rising left outside the wall containing the wood. Quickly joining a firmer cart track rising from the farm road, keep left on this to cross a gentle brow revealing Malham Tarn ahead. This runs grandly on to meet a stony access road near the tarn shore beneath the gleaming cliff of Great Close Scar.

Double back left on this to a gate back onto the open moor. Now leave the track and bear right on a grassy path, past the wood corner just ahead. Keep right on the path above the tarn shore to quickly reach Tarn Foot, where Malham Water emerges. At some 1230ft/375m above sea-level, Malham Tarn's unlikely existence in limestone country is due to a bed of harder Silurian slate. With its adjacent wetlands, the tarn is home to much bird-life, and the surrounding grassland, woodland and limestone pavement contribute to its status as a National Nature Reserve. Conclude by following the main path left the short way back to the car park.

Great Close Scar and Malham Tarn

3   MALHAM COVE

4¾ miles from Malham

Exploring the dry valley above the dramatic scenery of Malham Cove

Start *Village centre (SD 900626; BD23 4DA), National Park car park*
Map *OS Explorer OL2, Yorkshire Dales South/West*

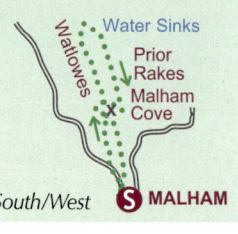

From the Centre pass through the village, keeping left at the junction by the bridge. After the final buildings at Town Head (featuring the National Trust's Town Head Barn), take a bridle-gate outside the farm/campsite on the right. With majestic Malham Cove in full view, a hugely popular and very durable path leads through the fields to the very foot of the massive limestone cliff rising 300 feet from the valley: issuing from the base is Malham Beck. To progress further, retrace steps a little to climb firm steps round the left side of the Cove. A kissing-gate at the top leads to an extensive limestone pavement. Though fascinating to tread, care must be taken on crossing it, for the grikes in between have very obvious leg-damaging capabilities.

At the end of the pavement at the centre of the Cove top a wall is met, and its near side is followed away from the Cove into Watlowes, the Dry Valley. After an intervening wall the crags on either side close in as you proceed along the flat valley floor, while Comb Hill and Dean Moor Hill form impressive portals at its head. At the dramatic valley-head the path climbs left to a stile, then swings sharp right on a ledge under Dean Moor Hill, looking back down on Watlowes. Soon the outcrops are left behind and a wall provides unerring company to Water Sinks. Here the outflow from Malham Tarn, for its brief existence known as Malham Water, disappears underground. It does not return to the surface again for more than two miles, at Aire Head Springs (see Walk 6).

Leave Water Sinks by retracing steps a few yards to a stile in the wall, and a path doubles gently back up onto Prior Rakes, an extensive sheep pasture recalling the landowning interests of Fountains Abbey. You quickly reach a junction alongside some pools, dewponds created in monastic times to help slake the thirsts of cattle in these largely dry limestone uplands. Turn right here alongside the pools, and a broad path rises gently to a hidden stile in the next wall. From here you pass through the well-defined trench of Trougate between low limestone outcrops. Through an old wall and then down to a ladder-stile in the next wall, another path junction is reached. Turn right down the wallside to a bridle-gate in the wall from earlier at the top of Malham Cove.

Re-cross the pavement and return to the foot of the Cove. Use the path back to Malham as far as the first gate, shortly after which cross the beck on a clapper-type footbridge. From a small gate behind, a path slants right up the slope then bears right on a level course to ruinous Bombeys Barn. Continuing on with a wall to a gateway, across the next field is a kissing-gate leading to a network of low walls, archaeologically valuable remains of Iron Age field boundaries. The now intermittently enclosed path passes through them and along to the head of a narrow, enclosed grassy footway. Bear right on its super course between walls to re-enter Malham in style. Emerging onto a back lane, continue straight down past the youth hostel into the centre.

On Malham Cove

4 GORDALE SCAR

4¾ miles from Malham

Easy walking to see the most dramatic limestone scenery in the Dales

Start *Village centre (SD 900626; BD23 4DA), National Park car park*
Map *OS Explorer OL2, Yorkshire Dales South/West*

From the Centre head into the village, quickly crossing Malham Beck on a footbridge at the forge and doubling back downstream. At a bridle-gate a firm path heads across the fields to a double kissing-gate. Here the path swings left to Mires Barn, crossing to the left of the wall to continue. The path remains firm throughout, always on the near side of Gordale Beck, which appears intermittently. When the beck is fully joined you shadow it upstream on a flagged section, and one last pasture leads to a kissing-gate into a delightful section of woodland. Scented with springtime wild garlic, a lovely stroll leads upstream to the charming waterfall of Janet's Foss. Legend has it that Janet, a local fairy queen, had a cave behind the falls. The water cascades into a clear green pool, the location of an ancient sheepwash. Here the path breaks off left to a kissing-gate onto the Gordale road.

Turn right a short distance, crossing the beck alongside an old bridge and often a refreshment van. You shall return to this point, but for now advance a little further to a gate on the left before Gordale House. Another hard path crosses the pasture to the waiting cliffs of Gordale Scar, converging as you enter within their dark confines. Gordale Scar is the most awe-inspiring of all Dales landmarks: unlike Malham Cove which bares all on first sighting, the intriguing Scar waits for the visitor to turn a final corner before impressing to the full. Once in its depths, the scale of the overhanging cliffs can be almost too daunting to fully appreciate the waterfalls: the upper one spills spectacularly through a circular hole in the rocks. Like the Cove it was formed by erosive action of ice and glacial meltwater.

Returning to the old bridge, leave by a kissing-gate sending a path to a wall corner just above. Now ascend the field to another such gate, then rise again to one atop steps at the top corner. Here a firm path runs left, remaining with the wall beneath open limestone country. At the end it slants up to the right to parallel the Malham Tarn road before joining it. Cross to a stile by a gate and a broad, grassy path heads away for a splendid upland stroll. A wall is joined and followed as far as the next corner. When the wall turns away, keep left to slant down towards the limestone pavement crowning Malham Cove immediately below. Drop to a bridle-gate to access the top of the Cove. Watlowes, the Dry Valley, strikes off right. The extensive pavement is fascinating to tread, but with caution as the grikes in between have leg-damaging capabilities: care is also needed as the mighty cliff of Malham Cove falls 300ft to the valley!

Cross to the far end, where a kissing-gate sends a stepped path down the steep slope beyond the Cove. At the bottom bear left to visit the very base of the mighty cliff: issuing quietly from it is Malham Beck, having sunk on the moor high above. To finish turn downstream with the beck on a broad, firm path through the fields to emerge onto the road on the village edge.

Gordale Scar

5 AROUND PIKEDAW HILL

4¼ miles from Malham

Old mines and sweeping views in delightful country west of Malham

Start Village centre (SD 900626; BD23 4DA), National Park car park
Map OS Explorer OL2, Yorkshire Dales South/West

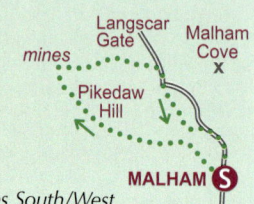

From the Centre turn right, away from the village and along a walled track. Almost at once fork right, and remain on this (passing a grassy way left) as far as a major junction. Turn left to ascend the walled lane, with a first view of Malham Cove. The track swings right at the top to rise more gently to a waterworks building. At this fork bear left, still on the main way passing barns with Kirkby Fell and Pikedaw Hill ahead. Their contrasting appearance is due to the Mid Craven Fault tracing the course of the beck and giving a transition from sombre gritstone to gleaming limestone.

The lane drops to a ford and slab footbridge. Across, go left a few yards and take a stile on the right. Cross the field (re-crossing the stream) to a wall-stile behind Butterlands Barn at the end. With the stream close by, a sustained uphill section begins by heading directly away. Bear slightly right to join a grassy way running to old workings, then rise the short way further to a stile/gate in the wall above. An intermittent path continues beneath Hoober Edge's limestone scars, with an old wall on your right. Rising pleasantly, cross the stream at a quad bike track but then rise right to a knoll, a decent path rising past lead mining spoil: a little further, down to your right is a stone-arched level, its keystone dated 1872.

Just above is a stile in a sturdy wall beneath Pikedaw Hill's top up to the right. Resume on a thin path straight up the slope ahead, beneath limestone scars yet looking across to Kirkby Fell's gritstone boulders. During a steeper pull the path swings right to quickly ease on grassy moorland. Penyghent makes an appearance through a gap ahead as the path ascends gently in the direction of

14

Nappa Gate on the skyline. A little higher you reach a sizeable pool on your left, just past which you meet a track that served adjacent mines: chief target of this early 19th century activity was calamine, a zinc ore. Turn right for 100 yards to join the Settle bridleway alongside a mineshaft guarded by a metal cover. Malham Tarn is well seen from this point just short of Nappa Gate.

Begin the return by descending the bridleway's superb, grassy course unfailingly down to a road, passing through just one intervening wall-gate. From the limestone surrounds en route, enjoy views to Malham Cove and village. From the gate onto the road turn right downhill as far as a sharp bend. From a gate in front a grassy track heads away, dropping to a gate at the head of grassy Long Lane. Advance down this broad pathway, through a dip and rising slightly to a level section. Here take a wall-stile on the left and drop down the field to join a wall. With super views to the Cove, note also the wall patterns of the the fields opposite. A little lower you pass through a gateway close to attractive High Barn. Continue down to a stile below, but don't jump through: on the other side sturdy steps ease you down into a considerably lower field. Slant right down through boulders to a gate onto the road on the edge of the village, going right to finish.

Looking back from beneath Pikedaw

6 AIRE HEAD SPRINGS

3½ miles from Malham

Gentle fieldpaths lead to a lovely finish on the bank of the newly formed River Aire

Start Village centre (SD 900626; BD23 4DA), National Park car park
Map OS Explorer OL2, Yorkshire Dales South/West

From the Centre turn away from the village along a walled track. At the immediate junction keep left, and with Kirkby Fell and Pikedaw ahead, this remains your course rising away to drop to a ford and slab bridge. The way then rises pleasantly to end at a gate alongside the barn conversion at Hall Close. An enclosed grass track rises towards Tranlands Barn ahead, but on levelling out well before reaching it, take a fence-stile on the right and rise left up a large, sloping pasture. From a stile/gate in the top wall corner, a grass track advances the short way to a streamlet crossing by a barn. Through an adjacent gate/stile ascend by the left-hand wall to a gate/stile on the brow. With Acraplatts Farm just ahead, cross the field to drop to a streamlet/stile above a wooded gill.

Continue on well beneath the farm to a fence-gate accessing tree-lined Tranlands Gill. From a slate footbridge rise past a ruin to a slim wall-stile above, then continue up to another scant ruin. Alongside is a stile/gate onto the farm road. The walk's high point affords views over much of Malhamdale, including the Cove. Turn left on the farm road to join a road, and left down its steep but quiet course: Kirkby Malham's imposing church tower soon appears below. At the village edge take an unsigned lane right, curving round past the old vicarage and church to a crossroads at the Victoria pub. For a note on Kirkby Malham see page 18.

Crossing straight over, advance as far as a rough lane left: this leads to the road at the northern edge of the village. Without joining it, take a wall-stile on the right. Head away into the field,

16

rising by the wall before swinging right across to a wall-stile opposite. A path continues over a sloping field, at the end revealing Scalegill Mill by the Aire. Through a stile the old millworkers' path slants down a grassy rake to join the drive in front of the now private dwelling. A mill has occupied this site since the Domesday Book, used in turn for processing corn, wool, flax and cotton.

Don't enter but take a bridle-gate on the left to pass round the outside, and a good path continues alongside the mill-cut and on above a millpond. Through a bridle-gate above a weir, advance to a wall-stile with a small spring in front: immediately over it are the emerging waters of Aire Head Springs. Here is the resurgence of a stream that last saw daylight at Water Sinks, high on the moor. It is not, therefore, the source of the Aire, but it is certainly the first naming of the river. Almost immediately downstream, its waters join the newly merged Malham and Gordale Becks to flow in unison as the Aire. Continue on to a kissing-gate, and ignoring the sewage works access road heading left, advance to a streamlet footbridge and kissing-gate just ahead. Keep on through two further fields alongside Malham Beck to emerge at a stile opposite the National Park Centre.

Aire Head Springs

7   KIRKBY MALHAM

4½ miles from Airton

A superb riverbank start leads to a historic village and concludes with wide views over Malhamdale

Start Village centre (SD 902591; BD23 4AL), roadside parking
Map OS Explorer OL2, Yorkshire Dales South/West

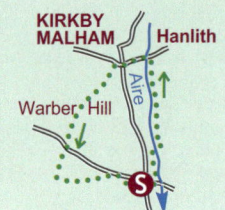

Airton is a tidy village with many old houses tucked away: main feature is the triangular green with its 'Squatter's House'. Alongside are the stone posts of the village stocks, while at the village edge is a farm shop/tearoom. From the green's eastern end descend towards the river, between a cottage with dovecotes and a 1696 datestone, and a Friends' Meeting House of 1700. Before dropping to the bridge, turn into the car park at the converted mill. From a bridle-gate at the end a path runs above the river, over a footbridge by the embankment of a mill-cut. At the end this is bridged to continue to a couple of kissing-gates, then across to a wall-stile from where a green way drops to a footbridge on the Aire.

Across it, advance to a tiny footbridge. Don't cross but turn upstream, the length of the field to regain the riverbank at twin bridle-gates. The Aire leads splendidly upstream, entering the parkland of Hanlith Hall. Keep straight on to a wall-stile onto the road at Hanlith Bridge, crossing it to follow the road into Kirkby Malham. Go straight over the crossroads past the Victoria pub with its 1840 sundial to reach the church of St Michael the Archangel. In its yard is the base of an old preaching cross, near the lych-gate are old stocks, while just past it is the imposing old vicarage.

Opposite the church a path runs to a slab bridge on Kirkby Beck, and steps up the other side lead up to a kissing-gate. Bear right across the field bottom, rising gently away to the foot of a line of trees. Steeply ascend the near side, with big views back over the church. This section of path is 'Kirk Gait', the old churchgoers' path from Otterburn. Across a track and stile at the top, a thin trod crosses to the far corner of a large field where a grassy, stone-arched footbridge crosses a streamlet to a wall-stile. Ascend the wallside towards Warber Hill, reaching a stile on the brow. Pendle Hill appears ahead, with Malham Cove behind you. Head away past a walled copse, angling steadily down to merge with the wall on the left. Noting the large limekiln in the pasture over to your left, continue down to a stile onto Scosthrop Lane.

From a stile opposite bear gently left, rising slightly across a brow to an outer wall corner. Continue with the wall on your left to a stile in an inner corner beyond, and yards further take another on the left. Cross to a clump of larches on a small quarry site, and continue to a gate in the wall ahead near tiny Dowber Laithe. Continue over a gentle brow and bear left down to the corner, where a gate by sheep pens sees you back onto Scosthrop Lane. Turn right to the first bend, then go right along the short drive to a house. Continue past it through a gate and head along the fenceside to another, where resume with a wall on your left. At the far end pass through a gate and across a small paddock onto a road at Town End. Go left to finish.

Kirkby Malham

8 RIVER AIRE

4½ miles from Airton

A splendid old lane leads to a sleepy hamlet and gentle riverside paths

Start Village centre (SD 902591; BD23 4AL), roadside parking
Map OS Explorer OL2, Yorkshire Dales South/West

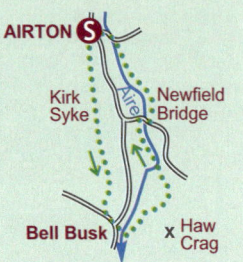

For a note on Airton see page 18. From the green cross the main road and head along the Hellifield road to a small green at a junction. Go left to quickly leave the village, and as the road swings left, bear right on the Kirk Syke Farm drive. At the farm keep straight on, over a ford/footbridge on this enclosed track rising to barns. Continuing, at a gate a little further you run grassily on a wallside, then through a gate to pass an old quarry and Well Head Laithe. The now grassy track crosses a field to a gate ahead, with the fence switching to the left to reach the next gate, in a wall. With Bell Busk just ahead, follow a fence down to a barn, behind which is a bridge over Otterburn Beck. From it a clear track leads through unkempt surrounds onto a road in the scattered settlement of Bell Busk, emerging alongside 17th century Raven Flatts.

Go left to a junction at Red Bridge on the beck, across which leave the Airton road by an access road right, crossing a large bridge over the River Aire. When this forks just beyond, take the left branch to a white-walled house. Pass around the back to a gate into a small paddock, across which a second gate puts you on the riverbank. Trace a grassy track upstream, and when the adjacent wall turns right, go with it. Through an intervening fence-gate trace the wall up past High Laithe to a gate at the top, with an old quarry to the right. Take the track slanting left, soon levelling to pass through a gateway on your right. Head away left past sheep feeders to a gentle brow on the grassy pasture of Eshton

Moor, where the walk's summit enjoys big Malhamdale views. A thin trod resumes left, over a broader green way and down to a gate/stile in the wall ahead. Just yards in front you join the largely invisible Pennine Way, which will be traced back to Airton.

Bear left on the gentlest of hollows down the centre of this vast field, with the winding Aire your target directly ahead. Also visible ahead is Newfield Hall. At the tapering bottom corner the path passes through neighbouring gates as it is squeezed between wall and road down to a streamlet, Tarn Dike. Downstream, a stile in the wall sends a briefly enclosed section to a wooden footbridge on the Aire. Across, turn upstream for a nice stroll to Newfield Bridge. En route you pass in and out of the base of a low wooded bank, emerging to see the bridge ahead. A clearer path forms to run to the wood end, where a fence deflects you right towards the bridge. A stile in it precedes one in the wall onto the road. Cross the bridge and take a stile on the left to resume upstream. After a stile you trace a wall to rejoin the river at the end, where adjacent stiles send you briefly away again to a wall-stile into a larger pasture. Here the pleasant path gradually returns to the riverbank for the final short stroll to a stile and steps onto the road at Airton Bridge. Cross it to climb back up into the village.

The River Aire at Newfield Bridge

9   LANGBER LANE

4¾ miles from Long Preston

Delightful paths and a green lane in a quiet corner of the Dales

Start *Village centre (SD 833582; BD23 4PH), roadside parking*
Map *OS Explorer OL2, Yorkshire Dales South/West*
or *Explorer OL41, Forest of Bowland & Ribblesdale*

    Long Preston is a pleasant village whose focal point is a green graced by a maypole and old milestone. Facing it is the Maypole Inn, with the Boars Head and a Post office/store nearby. St Mary's church has a low-slung roof and a Norman font. From the maypole green, head away from the main road along School Lane. Just past a junction behind the school, a walled grassy path heads off left to join and follow New House Lane (for the church remain on the narrow road). The lane's gradually rougher surfaced course passes several houses until it turns sharp right through a gate. Instead use a gate in front, continuing as a pleasant grassy wallside way. Through a gate at the end an enclosed track rises to Little Newton.
    Keep left of the farm buildings to pens at the end, then from a gate on the left join the bank of Newton Gill. A shapely bridge carries you over it and an inviting grass track runs upstream. Approaching trees, the track rises above the stream, looking down on the tilted strata of Waterfall Rock and a minor waterfall. Here go straight ahead on a thin trod left of a projecting wall to a stile onto a corner of grassy Newton Moor. A little path drops to follow the beck beneath newly planted trees. At a confluence and wall corner you swing right, and with beck and wall down to the left, the improved path slowly rises through embryo trees towards a fence-gate on the brow. Ideally fork left before it to a wall junction, with a stile and tiny footbridge hidden in front. Across, go briefly left up the wallside to a stile. A grassy way slants right up a vast,

reedy pasture, fading before you pass through a fence-gate just short of a wall-corner. Maintain this line, crossing a ditch to a stile onto Langber Lane. Turn left on this old green way, becoming firmer at the house at Bookilber Barn. Ingleborough is briefly seen ahead, while to the left are Pendle Hill and the Bowland moors.

Leave when the track drops down to Bookil Gill Beck: a thin path doubles back sharp left to a gate. A few yards downstream ford the beck, and a delightful green path heads away. As the beck drops left in lively fashion, the path contours right away from it, crossing to an old wall before a couple of trees. Past them the path drops through successive gates and bears left onto a spur above a confluence. Through a gate cross the right-hand footbridge on Long Preston Beck to a track slanting up the bank to a gate/stile at the top of the tiny New Pasture Plantation. Just yards beyond a stile into the wood, take another to forsake the track. Aim diagonally away from the corner, on the brow locating a stile ahead: the village now appears below you. Descend to another stile, and from one just below, further obvious stiles lead your thin path diagonally across more fields to a stile beyond a fenced reedy pool. Two final fields are crossed to a corner-stile onto Green Gate Lane. Go left to finish.

The maypole and the Maypole Inn

10　　　　　　　　　　　　　　　CLEATOP PARK

4 miles from Settle

Colourful country and massive views on the lesser known side of Settle

Start *Town centre (SD 819636; BD24 9EJ), car parks*
Map *OS Explorer OL2, Yorkshire Dales South/West* **or** *Explorer OL41, Forest of Bowland & Ribblesdale*

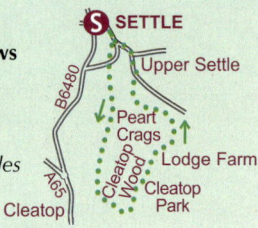

For a note on Settle see page 26. Facing the arched Shambles, bear right to the corner of the Market Place and along a road past a bank, then on High Street past the Talbot Arms to Chapel Street. Cross over along Chapel Square to Greenfoot car park, where a tarmac path crosses grassy swards on its left side. Towards the end pass through a wall-gap, between housing at Lower Greenfoot and out onto a road. Just a few yards right, go left on the walled track of Brockhole Lane, passing allotments as you leave town.

Shortly reaching a stream, a path shadows it the short way to its exit under a wall-arch. Your way narrows to a footway, and ignoring a branch left at a kissing-gate, simply trace this course to emerge onto unsurfaced Lodge Road by barns at Hoyman Laithe. From a stile opposite cross a field to a corner wall-stile, then a modest path forms to rise to a stile just ahead. Resume with a wall on your left, a small path later forming to run to a corner wall-stile behind trees into the Woodland Trust's Cleatop Wood. During this stage enjoy views over the Ribble Valley and back to Ingleborough.

A path heads away across largely open country, dropping gently to a wall-stile at the end. The path resumes across partly wooded terrain, rapidly reaching a gate on the left at the start of a wood. Passing through into Cleatop Park, an excellent path slants right through it, a sustained but steady gradient through springtime bluebells to ease at a bend near the wood edge. Here the path doubles sharply back left at an easier gradient, soon levelling out at the wood top. On the brow the path bears right a few yards to a wall-stile, emerging into a massive reedy pasture with big views to Settle and Penyghent, rapidly joined by Ingleborough.

A thin path slants down across it, bound for Lodge Farm at the far side. Crossing two streamlets the vague path curves around to run with a wall to a corner gate. A few yards further is the farm, where bear right on a walled track. Briefly level, it rises to a gate into Hudsa Plantation. Soon easing, as an improving cart track it takes a gate out of the trees and past colourful Peart Crags on your left. Rising gently outside new woodland, it swings left to reach a gate. Though a stony track leads onto an old road ahead, you take a ladder-stile on the left. A grand path heads away with a wall on your right through moor-grass, further on dropping past scattered boulders to a wall-stile just short of the corner. Superb views look over town to a landscape overseen by Ingleborough.

A thin path heads away, dropping more steeply at the end to a small gate overlooking a steep drop. A thin path turns right to slant down the wallside, near the end passing through a gate for a few enclosed yards to another, then along a wallside to a gate onto Mitchell Lane. Turn left to the fringe of Upper Settle, meeting a through road at a little green by a former chapel. Go left down through characterful corners to emerge by The Folly, a rambling 17th century house with an intricate façade: it incorporates the Museum of North Craven Life. The centre is a minute further.

Settle from under Peart Crags

11 THE SETTLE HILLS

4 miles from Settle

An enthralling exploration of limestone heights overlooking Settle

Start *Town centre (SD 819636; BD24 9EJ), car parks*
Map *OS Explorer OL2, Yorkshire Dales South/West*
or *Explorer OL41, Forest of Bowland & Ribblesdale*

Settle is a busy little town, focal point for an extensive rural area. Tuesday markets present a lively scene when the small square is awash with colour. Facing the square is the historic Shambles, with shops peeping from behind archways, and also a former inn the 'Naked Man', with its entertaining sign of 1633. Nearby is The Folly, a rambling 17th century house with an intricate façade, home to the Museum of North Craven Life. Also of note are the Town Hall (1833), Victoria Hall (1853) and Friends' Meeting House (1689). Leave the market place by Constitution Hill, left of the Shambles. After a steep pull the road turns left: almost at once abandon it in favour of the rougher Banks Lane to the right. This restored path climbs between walls to emerge into open country. Big views look back over Settle and Giggleswick to the Bowland moors, while Ingleborough appears before the lane ends.

At once the way forks: take the right branch slanting up the bank, through an old wall then turning to ascend more directly. Joined by a wall from the left it rises steeply to a gate at the top. Keep on, an early fork giving alternative options on broad grassy paths that will shortly merge. Now level, the stunning scenery of Warrendale Knotts and Attermire Scar appears ahead. The path drops into this upland bowl by way of two old walls, over a stile and on past an old shooting range to a gateway below Attermire Scar. Attermire Cave is a dark slit high up the limestone cliff.

Through the gateway take the wallside path rising left to a nick, then on a fine green way through a trough: Ingleborough and Whernside fill the view ahead. A wall joins you to rise to a kissing-gate, and a thinner path resumes alongside the wall beneath scree at the foot of a limestone scar. The entrance to Victoria Cave can be gleaned by the clean rockface above it, and a thin path detours up to it - be wary of potential rockfalls. The massive entrance has been blasted to this size in modern times, but it has yielded bones of rhinoceros, hippopotamus, bear, mammoth and Stone Age man. Another path slants back down to the main one, rising gently to a brow. Just beyond is a kissing-gate onto unsurfaced Gorbeck Road.

Turn left through the gate and descend the track to join the steep road out of Langcliffe. Just before reaching it, Penyghent appears impressively up Ribblesdale. At once take a gate on the left and head away on a splendid path, passing beneath a wood and above a steep fall to the valley. Two intervening bridle-gates are met before the path curves down a big sloping pasture, with a minor limestone scar near the end, to a bridle-gate. Through this follow a wall away to merge with a lower bridleway a little further. Simply remain on this, briefly enclosed, then on to merge with the outward route to descend Banks Lane back into town.

Victoria Cave

12   AROUND LANGCLIFFE

$3^3{/}4$ miles from Settle

A lovely village sits amid absorbing features either side of the Ribble

Start *Town centre (SD 819636; BD24 9EJ), car parks*
Map *OS Explorer OL2, Yorkshire Dales South/West*
or *Explorer OL41, Forest of Bowland & Ribblesdale*

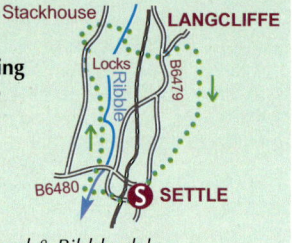

    For a note on Settle see page 26. From the Town Hall by the market place cross the main road and head down Kirkgate, passing Victoria Hall and the Friends' Meeting House. Under the railway pass Marshfield dating from 1780 on the right and straight on with a supermarket on the left. At the bend leave the road for a traffic-free way left of the fire station. Swing right on a road at the end to the rear of historic Kings Mill. Go left to a footbridge over the River Ribble and take a surfaced path upstream to the main road bridge.

    Cross the road and head straight off along an enclosed path between sports fields: ahead rises Penyghent. At the end join the river briefly before being ushered away into a field. Cross to a prominent stile to enjoy a brief section above a steep wooded riverbank: directly below is Langcliffe paper mill. Emerging again, bear left across the field to a stile onto Stackhouse Lane. Either turn right, or from a stile opposite avoid tarmac by going right on a parallel course along the field bottom, returning via another stile at the end. A little further is the edge of Stackhouse, a cosy grouping of exclusive dwellings huddled beneath the hillside in protective greenery. A short loop gives a slightly closer look: take the first rough road into it, turning first right along what becomes a grassy cart track, then right again back onto the road. Just yards further, take a walled path to the right to meet the Ribble at Locks, an attractive scene that incorporates a weir.

Across the footbridge turn right along a street between old millworkers' cottages. At the end a snicket runs left to an attractive millpond, and turn right on the path running along its full length. At the end the path swings left between pond and paper mill onto an access road. Go left to the junction ahead by a caravan park, then straight ahead on a walled path. This rises to bridge the railway up onto the valley road at Langcliffe. Cross to a side road opposite and along into the village centre. By the phonebox a tablet on a house depicts the Naked Woman, modestly dated 1660: once an inn, it was a close friend of Settle's more famous Naked Man.

Alongside the spacious green, remain on the road past the fountain and on between a former school and the church. As the road leaves the village by passing through a gateway prior to climbing away, instead take a gate to the right. A steep path ascends past a spring to a gate at the top, where bear right on a thin, lower path above a wall. Levelling out it gives a bird's-eye picture of Langcliffe with Ingleborough beyond, while up-dale, Penyghent overtops Stainforth Scar. At a bridle-gate advance to a gate/stile in another wall to merge with a bridleway from the left. On again, becoming briefly enclosed to drop down, Settle is laid out as on a map. Following a wall to a gate at the end, a restored path makes an enclosed descent of Banks Lane onto a back lane at the top of Constitution Hill. Turn left to drop down into the market place.

At Langcliffe

13   GIGGLESWICK SCAR

3¾ miles from Buckhaw Brow

Easy walking around varied limestone features

Start *Scar Top (SD 797658; BD24 0DJ), lay-by on B6480 summit opposite lone house*
Map *OS Explorer OL41, Forest of Bowland & Ribblesdale*

    Buckhaw Brow is a road climb that was an animated scene prior to Settle by-pass opening. From the lay-by the right-hand of two gates sends a path slanting left up through a limestone cleft atop Giggleswick Scar. Quickly levelling out to approach a bridle-gate in the adjacent wall, instead double back right on a thinner but clear path, quickly nearing an old wall to your right. Pendle Hill and Bowland's moors rise across the Ribble Valley. Dropping through a small limestone pavement advance beneath limestone scars high above the wooded main scar. Over a stile in a sturdy wall, the path runs on through increasingly enchanting surrounds.

    A second wall-stile is crossed, and just after a crumbled wall, a minor brow reveals Schoolboys Tower ahead. The path drops gently past a prominent cairn on a mound: a detour past it sends a trod 150 yards down to the tower, an enormous cairn erected long ago by Giggleswick School pupils. Beneath is the rim of a massive old quarry. Double back left, a path forming to rejoin the main one which runs well outside the quarry fence, passing a cairned knoll to reach a crumbling wall fronted by a small pavement. Turn sharp right between old wall and quarry fence to descend with an appreciation of the quarry's scale. Penyghent and Fountains Fell enter the scene back to the left across Ribblesdale.

    When wall and fence diverge, abandon the quarry for a path dropping more sharply nearer the wall. Towards the bottom of this big bowl double back left on a green way through the old wall. It crosses a large, sloping rough pasture, rising slightly to ascend through scattered trees. When a left branch curves uphill out of the trees, advance straight on to a wall corner just ahead. Follow the wall away until a stile admits to the wood. Go left to the edge of the trees, then slant down to the left-hand of two stiles in the wall ahead. A thin trod heads away to merge with a broader path from the other stile. Follow it up through the left-hand of two gates, from where it winds more steeply up to the left. Swinging right and levelling out it forks, though merges a short way further above an outer wall corner. It then runs to a gate in the facing wall just above an inner corner. Through it the grassy track heads away close by the right-hand wall, enjoying a brief glimpse of Ingleborough.

Through a gate just yards short of the far end is another path junction: go left to a gate in the wall corner and head off on a delightful, gently rising path. Beyond another gate this soon rises with a wall to bring Ingleborough into view. As the wall parts company continue to the next gate/stile, with Austwick appearing ahead. As the track gently descends Feizor Thwaite to a guidepost amid grassy paths, take one doubling back sharply left. It angles towards the nearby wall, and along to an inner corner gate. Head away with the wall, which soon turns off as your broad green way strikes across the pasture to a bridle-gate. It then rises more faintly to a bridle-gate on a brow. Head away to drop to the bridle-gate from five minutes into the walk, going right to finish as you began.

Giggleswick Scar

14   STAINFORTH FORCE

4 miles from Langcliffe

A feast of interest between two villages - too much for one walk!

Start Village centre (SD 822650; BD24 9NQ), car park at old school
Map OS Explorer OL2, Yorkshire Dales South/West **or** Explorer OL41, Forest of Bowland & Ribblesdale

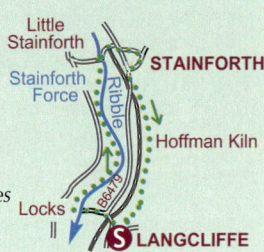

    Langcliffe is a lovely village with a spacious green. By the phonebox a tablet on a house depicts the Naked Woman, modestly dated 1660 and once an inn. Leave by a rough lane to the left of the old school north of the green: quickly reaching a junction, bear right on a walled track (Pike Lane) out of the village. Within minutes two paths go left: take the first, leaving a small gate to run an enclosed fieldside course down onto a walled track. Go briefly left to the B6479 and right over the parallel rail footbridge. Across the road, descend a short lane to old millworkers' cottages at Locks, where you meet the Ribble at an attractive scene with a weir.
    Across the footbridge ignore the enclosed path heading away, and turn upstream through a bridle-gate by the weir. Splendid riverbank walking leads along past an old paper mill on the other bank. At the end of a long pasture after it, a wooded bank with stiles at either end puts you high above the river: during this stage you pass a lively spring. The path runs on above a newly planted bank to a bridle-gate into open pasture. Approaching the river again, as a track forms at the end, instead take a bridle-gate on the right to trace the Ribble the short way to ever-popular Stainforth Force. Just beyond the supremely lovely falls you join a back road at 17th century Stainforth Bridge: cross and ascend the lane. Levelling out, a bridle-gate on the right before the rail bridge sends an enclosed path along to drop left to bridge the railway. Ignore a gate onto the road and take a bridle-gate right, dropping to a B6479 underpass

by Stainforth Beck. Emerging at Stainforth car park/WC, join the road, turn right to a junction, then right to the Craven Heifer.

Continue past the pub to the main road. A short way along the footway a stile sends a path across the field to bridle-gates enclosing a stream, then on through a gateway. Continue towards the next field-end where a fence-stile puts you into the environs of the old Craven Lime Works. Advance on through scattered trees to the old winding house, then down an incline and on to a slab bridge/stile revealing the Hoffman Kiln in front. Just before this, a short branch right reveals the massive triple draw kilns. Dropping to the Hoffman Kiln, this amazing structure of 1873 features 22 individual chambers, and occupied 90 workers at its peak.

At the far end drop into an open area. Pass left of a house and follow the access road out past a red-brick weigh-house. Just after this a short path detours left up to the remains of the Spencer Kilns. As the road swings right to pass under the railway to the valley road, instead take an enclosed cart track left of the line. Through a gate/stile at the end it rises gently towards a stile at the far side. The way continues across to a small gate in a fence, and on to another stile on a gentle brow: look back to appraise a fine prospect up the valley. Now bear left to a corner stile back onto Pike Lane, turning right to finish as you began.

The Ribble below Stainforth

15   CATRIGG FORCE

3½ miles from Stainforth

A secretive waterfall is highlight of a super limestone ramble

Start *Village centre (SD 821673; BD24 9PB), National Park car park*
Map *OS Explorer OL2, Yorkshire Dales South/West*
or *Explorer OL41, Forest of Bowland & Ribblesdale*

Stainforth stands high above and back from the Ribble, long since by-passed by the valley road. The Craven Heifer pub sports a popular local name, while St Peter's church dates from 1842. Stainforth's best known features, its packhorse bridge and waterfall on the Ribble are to be found outside the village (see Walk 14). Also on the village edge is the mansion of Taitlands, a youth hostel for around 60 years until 2007. With your back to the pub, head along a short back lane to an early junction. Go right a few strides and take a short drive left, signed to Winskill. Rising between houses, bear right to a gate/stile and rise into the field, slanting to a gate ahead. Now commence a greater slant up this extensive pasture, beneath a fence enclosing scrub at the foot of Stainforth Scar. Smearsett Scar is well seen across the valley, with Ingleborough beyond. Stay on the upper path closest to the fence, as part way up you use a kissing-gate in it. A limestone stepped path climbs concertedly through foliage to a ladder-stile at the top. Views look down the valley to Settle, with Pendle Hill beyond.

Head away on a path rising gently above the escarpment to a ladder-stile at the end. Both Whernside and Penyghent have by now appeared to complete the famous trio. The paths bears gently left over a brow to reveal Lower Winskill just below: drop left to another ladder-stile in the wall below. Head out between the buildings on the walled drive rising to the entrance to Upper Winskill Farm. Turn right on the surfaced access road which rises steadily across the open country of Winskill Stones: note a distinctive 'erratic' Silurian boulder perched on limestone just above. Joining the Malham Moor road at the top, a clear day calls for a pause to appraise Lakeland's distant Coniston Fells. Turn left on this unfenced strip of tarmac between limestone outcrops. An old limekiln sits on the right before the brow, which then reveals a fine skyline featuring Penyghent, Plover Hill and Fountains Fell.

Just before dropping to a cattle-grid, double back sharply left on a firm cart track, passing a crumbling limekiln. The track slants down through several rough pastures with Penyghent prominent to your right. Remain on this all the way down to a steeper drop into the bottom corner of a field with a prominent clump of trees behind: this is the location of Catrigg Force. Through the gate is the head of Goat Scar Lane. Before heading down it, first savour the waterfall detour. Through a small gate on the right a short path drops down to the top of the waterfall, where with great caution you can peer down to the bottom. A conventional view can be sampled by entering trees on the left to descend a good path to the foot of the ravine. Back on Goat Scar Lane, turn down its enclosed course all the way into Stainforth: mighty Ingleborough is dominant ahead for most of this stage. Emerging onto a green, drop right of it to cross some stepping-stones on Stainforth Beck in a lovely corner. From the smaller green across it, go left on the road back to the start.

Catrigg Force

16   SMEARSETT SCAR

4½ miles from Stainforth

A gentle ascent to a stunning viewpoint, with much interest en route

Start *Village centre (SD 821673; BD24 9PB), National Park car park*
Map *OS Explorer OL2, Yorkshire Dales South/West (tiny section on Explorer OL41, Forest of Bowland & Ribblesdale)*
Access *Section over Smearsett is Open Access, see page 4*

For a note on Stainforth see page 34. From the bottom corner of the car park a bridleway shadows Stainforth Beck through an underpass beneath the valley road, then turn right to a bridle-gate onto an access track. Go left on this to bridge the railway, then bear right on an enclosed path. This runs above the railway to a gate at the end onto a back lane. Go left for a swift descent to cross 17th century Stainforth Bridge, built to serve the York-Lancaster packhorse trade. Continue up to a junction at Little Stainforth, a hamlet also known as Knight Stainforth. Its three-storey hall dates largely from the 17th century, with a tearoom across the road.

Head up the farm drive directly opposite, continuing up the enclosed rough track to a wall-stile at the top: Penyghent has now entered the scene. A stony track rises away, fading in a vast, sloping pasture. Head directly up the centre, and on the brow pause to enjoy a big Ribblesdale prospect. Smearsett Scar appears ahead as you advance to a gate/stile. Continuing to a gentle brow, its profile extends to neighbouring Pot Scar, enclosing their hidden valley. The path slants left down to a ladder-stile just short of the corner. Though it runs invitingly on through this upland trough, advance only to the wall corner on your right, then turn right on a wallside path to another such stile beneath the crest of Smearsett Scar. A thin path ascends the wallside to a brow, from where strike left through the edge of the rocks up to the summit at 1191ft/363m.

Smearsett Scar has an OS column, a pile of stones and three shelters: on its south face, low crags give way to scree slopes. This is a prime spot for appraising the Ribblesdale landscape: included are Horton, Penyghent, Stainforth and Settle's inimitable hills. The broader panorama includes Pendle Hill, the Bowland moors and Ingleborough presiding over its limestone entourage. Leave by heading west on a thin trod above the edge, bound towards Pot Scar. Part way on, however, a scarp deflects you 'inland' close to a distinctive cairn: here continue slanting down the pasture on a fading grassy way to merge with a wall. A slight rise meets a broad, grassy path at a gate. Don't use it but turn right for a very gentle rise to a brow, continuing on to drop gently towards Ribblesdale. Approaching a wall it forks: take the right branch to a ladder-stile.

Drop slightly right to a wall-stile in the corner, and from one just beneath it drop down the side of a large field. From the gate at the far end a track runs down to a gate onto a road, but the right of way drops left to a gate at Hargreaves Barn, and an enclosed grassy way runs to the road at the same point. Turn right to Little Stainforth, and go left up a short driveway just before the hall. After a cottage with a sundial a stile puts you into a field. Slant right down to a stile in the wall before the bottom, back onto the outward lane. Finish as you began, though at Stainforth Bridge enjoy the delights of Stainforth Force downstream before concluding.

Pot Scar and Ingleborough from Smearsett Scar

17   FEIZOR'S WOODS

4 miles from Austwick

Delectable natural woodland amid idyllic limestone surroundings

Start Village centre (SD 767685; LA2 8BB), roadside parking
Map OS Explorer OL2, Yorkshire Dales South/West & Explorer OL41, Forest of Bowland & Ribblesdale
Access Woodland section is Open Access

    For a note on Austwick see page 40. From the green outside the Gamecock Inn turn down the narrow lane opposite, quickly taking a snicket right. Past the houses it runs on as a flagged path, concluding through a field to a stile onto a road on the village edge. Turn left to Austwick Bridge, across which go left on a walled track, Wood Lane. Where it bends left leave by a gate/stile on the right, crossing a long field to a stile onto a walled bridleway well right of Wood House. Cross over to climb a field to a stile on the brow. Pausing to appraise the view, Austwick nestles beneath Ingleborough, while Robin Proctor's Scar projects beneath Norber and its boulderfield: ahead, Feizor is revealed beneath Pot Scar.

    From the stile a largely pathless but obvious march ensues through a string of fields with Oxenber and Feizor Woods to the left. Stiles come thick and fast towards the end, maintaining a near-straight line to enter the hamlet of Feizor across a stream. Go left past the popular tearoom, swinging left past a pump and trough to the last houses. Through a gate the narrow road climbs away, with big views over your outward route to the Bowland moors. Swinging right, it eases out as a track to rise through a hollow to the gap of Feizor Nick. Penyghent suddenly appears majestically ahead.

    Dropping slightly to pass through a gate, within yards take a stile left into Wharfe Wood's Open Access land. A springtime bluebell carpet extends through both this and Oxenber Wood. The ensuing route through these woods follows two recommended paths with regular marker posts: ignore any lesser branches. A path meanders away through scrubby trees, soon swinging left up to a clearing on a knoll. Here it bears right to run close by a wall on the left. With intermittent views to Ingleborough the path gently declines into denser trees to reach a corner wall-stile. This puts you into Oxenber Wood, and the path drops slightly into more open surrounds. Soon swinging left, it rises gently to run through open terrain amid scattered limestone. Soon entering a vast clearing, a junction of the two main paths is reached in this gentle hollow. Double back right, soon descending into colourful open pasture.

Ahead is Wharfe beneath Moughton, with Ingleborough dominant beyond. Dropping towards a clump of trees, the path swings left beneath it and down through bracken to a path and wall. Go left through a gate/stile, and the green path drops down with the wall to neighbouring gates at the bottom. Leaving Open Access land, a short walled path drops down onto another walled way, Wood Lane again. Just a few yards left take a stile on the right and descend the field to a stile at the very bottom. This puts you onto a walled bridleway. Turn right to a ford at Flascoe Bridge: this clapper bridge on Austwick Beck gives a splendid final moment. Across, the way soon broadens out and runs on to the road on the edge of the village, going left to finish.

Oxenber Wood

18   CRUMMACK DALE

3¾ miles from Austwick

Supremely easy walk amid truly beautiful limestone scenery

Start *Village centre (SD 767685; LA2 8BB), roadside parking*
Map *OS Explorer OL2, Yorkshire Dales South/West*

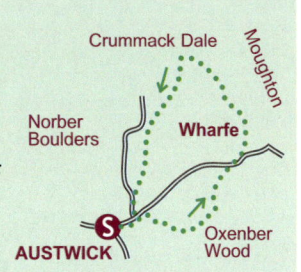

Austwick is an attractive village with a small green, the cosy Gamecock Inn, an old hall, shop and tidy cottages. The tiny church of the Epiphany with its little bell-cote sits at the green junction. From the green outside the pub, head east out of the village, away from the centre. Beyond the last houses an enclosed bridleway turns off right to reach Flascoe Bridge and a ford on Austwick Beck. At this charming spot you cross the first of the day's two clapper bridges. Continuing, almost at once take a stile on the left into a field. Rise to a stile in the top left corner to join another enclosed way, Wood Lane. Turn left on its lovely course, broadening to run along by Wood End Farm and out onto a road. Go right for a couple of minutes, then turn left by a barn up an enclosed old lane that ascends gently into the hamlet of Wharfe.

When the tarmac ends, ignore a right fork and rise straight on between houses the short way to another junction. Swing left for a few yards then turn up a cart track right: just a few strides further left is the lovely Manor House of 1715. Wharfe is an improbable chocolate box settlement, hidden from the outside world by leafy lanes that function only as bridleways. Back at the track it immediately climbs out of the hamlet as White Stone Lane. This is followed for some time, initially in a deep, sunken course. Beyond a couple of barns it narrows and eases further to run a magnificent course into Crummack Dale. High above you are the gleaming limestone scars that seam Moughton's flanks.

Eventually becoming track width again, just a minute further is a fork: bear left on the track down to a superb clapper bridge and ford on Austwick Beck. This is a grand spot, complete with a seat and stone slab bridge: the pool here was known as Wash Dub, once dammed by farmers to dip sheep to scrub them of parasites. Very shortly after crossing, take a small, hidden gateway on the left and trace the wall the short way to a stile in it. In the field behind, rise directly past scattered Silurian rocks, fading before finding a wall-stile on the brow. Pause to look back over the great stretch of Crummack Dale framed between Norber and Moughton, while ahead is a massive new view to Pendle Hill and Bowland's moors.

Head directly away on a faint green way down across a large stony pasture to Sowerthwaite Farm drive. Ideally you'll meet it with a wall-stile directly behind: if not, turn briefly right to locate it. Cross the field to the next wall-stile, then advance to the near wall corner. Ignoring a stile onto Crummack Lane, drop straight down to a slab bridge on Norber Sike and on to a stile just ahead. Now rise to a corner stile onto a rough lane, crossing straight over and along and down the wallside to a stile into a garden. The way runs straight down between houses onto Townhead Lane. Turn down to the bottom and go right for the village centre.

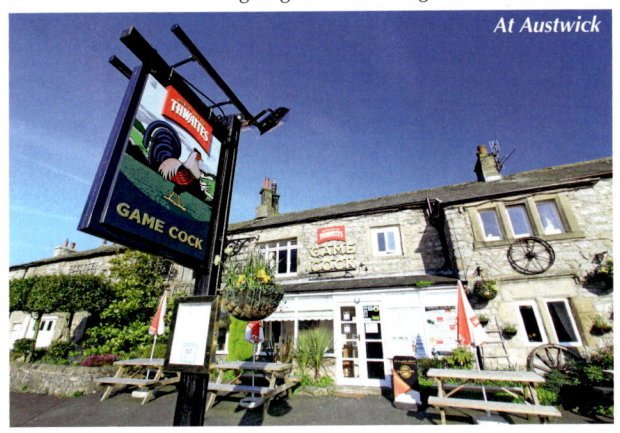

At Austwick

19 LONG LANE

3¾ miles from Helwith Bridge

An old green lane leads to big views and unsung paths in the heart of Ribblesdale

Start Hamlet centre (SD 810695; BD24 0EH), car park
Map OS Explorer OL2, Yorkshire Dales South/West

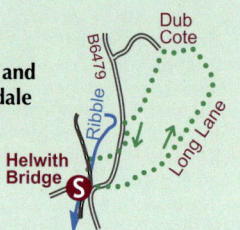

The Helwith Bridge Hotel is a welcoming riverside pub, while the bridge itself spans both the River Ribble and the Settle-Carlisle Railway. It regularly groans under the weight of waggons serving quarries that dominate here. Cross the bridge to a junction with the B6479, and go left a few yards before branching right up a walled track, Moor Head Lane. Briefly steep and stony, it quickly improves to rise and run on to a fork. Bear left to commence a long, easy march up the splendid green way of Long Lane, with Penyghent drawing you on ahead. All the Three Peaks are visible, while looking back, Pendle Hill joins a long Bowland skyline.

When the walls depart and a single fence takes over, the track continues up to a gate in a cross-wall. Only five minutes beyond this, as the main route forges on more steeply towards Penyghent, branch off left on a level, mercurially surfaced grassy way through a gap in the crumbling wall. With Horton-in-Ribblesdale outspread on the valley floor below, the path slants down to a gate/stile in the bottom corner. Continue down, a thinner grassy way curving away from the wall to return at a gate in the corner. The descent concludes past Dub Cote, which offers bunkbarn accommodation.

Alongside the barn, ignore the surfaced access road right, and turn left on a firm access road. When it swings left up to Newlands House, keep straight on the inviting green way's walled course to White Sike Barn. Through the gate take a wall-stile in front, and drop down to cross a streamlet before swinging right to a ladder-stile in a wall. Bear left down the large field to a wall-stile just above the stream. Descend the wallside, crossing the stream three further times outside the confines of the first barn to reach a ladder-stile in the bottom corner. Turn down the access track past modern barns the short way to a gate at New Barn onto the B6479.

Don't join the main road but go left on a section of old road. When it rejoins the road cross and follow the verge left a short way to a wall-stile on your right opposite Middle Studfold Farm, with tearoom. Cross the field to a stile at the start of the wall ahead, and follow it away until it swings round to the left: here advance across the field to a footbridge on the River Ribble. Across, go left on an enclosed path away from the river, briefly stone-flagged to reach an enclosed cart track. This runs left to pass beneath the railway onto an access road. Cross to a kissing-gate opposite and follow the enclosed path left to avoid quarry waggons on the parallel road. When it rejoins the road, cross to a kissing-gate and bear right across two small fields towards the pub. To the left, a low viaduct makes a fine foreground to Penyghent. A final ladder-stile puts you into the pub car park.

Ingleborough from above Dub Cote

20 SULBER NICK

4¾ miles from Horton-in-Ribblesdale

Remote paths and popular paths meet on the limestone flanks of Ingleborough

Start *Village centre (SD 807726; BD24 0HE), National Park car park*
Map *OS Explorer OL2, Yorkshire Dales South/West*
Access *Open Access, see page 4*

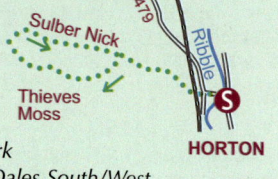

For a note on Horton see page 46. From the Penyghent Café head briefly north into the car park and past the WC to cross the footbridge at its northern end to by-pass the road bridges by the Crown Hotel. Over the Ribble remain on the roadside footway to a junction at the end. Go straight ahead up a driveway towards the station, taking a small gate to the left onto the platform. Until the new footbridge is in place, cross the line with care and a little path rises to a kissing-gate into a field. The path crosses to a small gate just ahead, with the farm at Beecroft Hall appearing. Bear right, the firm path crossing a large field to the farm drive, with a bridle-gate in the wall just beyond. The path crosses another large field, swinging left further on and up to a bridle-gate into a sloping limestone pasture. Here you enter Open Access land within Ingleborough National Nature Reserve. The partially cairned path slants right, levels out and repeats this formula, to then cross to a gateway in an old wall. It heads away to fork 150 yards further.

Keep straight on the Ingleborough path, rising to a cairn on a knoll then along to a bridle-gate in a wall just ahead. You shall return to this point to finish, but for now leave the path by rising left alongside the wall. Ingleborough makes its majestic appearance to your right, and will remain the centrepiece for the next near-mile. Follow the wall along the short way to where a fence joins it, and turn right with the fence. An inviting grass track rapidly forms, close to the fence. After a short while it splits, but remain on the initially more vague left branch to keep faith with the fence. This it successfully does throughout its length, running a splendid level course above a limestone escarpment overlooking the plateau of Thieves Moss. Latterly a distant Pendle Hill slots into view. At the far end the errant branch returns for the short stroll to meet the Austwick-Selside bridleway as it comes through a gate in the wall just to the left. Turn right on this for a few minutes' stroll to Sulber path crossroads.

Here the path ascending Ingleborough from Horton crosses over the Austwick-Selside bridleway. Rejoining the Ingleborough path, turn right on its course through the distinct trough of Sulber Nick. The wayward staggering of Three Peaks walkers nearing the end of their marathon is evident in the state of the path after a wet spell. Looking back, Ingleborough quickly returns to view. At the end of the nick it drops down to rejoin the outward route at the bridle-gate from earlier. Passing through, all that remains is to retrace steps back to Horton, now fully savouring the awesome picture of Penyghent straight ahead.

Penyghent from Sulber

21 AROUND HORTON

3¼ miles from Horton-in-Ribblesdale

A steady stroll around the outskirts of Horton by way of riverbank, beck, old lane and a fine ravine

Start Village centre (SD 807726; BD24 0HE), National Park car park
Map OS Explorer OL2, Yorkshire Dales South/West

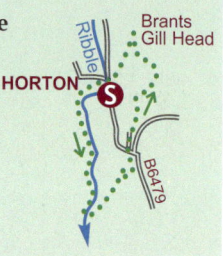

    Horton-in-Ribblesdale is the first village on the Ribble, and is the centre of Three Peaks country. It has little intrinsic charm, being a curious mixture of dwellings strung along the road, though 17th century datestones adorn some cottage lintels. Horton's real attraction is its location: there is a true walkers' atmosphere here. It has a campsite and a renowned cafe, while pubs are found at either end. The Crown has two arched bridges outside, while the Golden Lion faces St Oswald's church with its Norman doorway. From the Penyghent Café head north into the car park, and past the WC cross the footbridge beyond it to by-pass the narrow road bridges by the Crown. Immediately across the Ribble, take a stile on the left to follow the river downstream. The Ribble provides company for a super mile's stroll that includes a section of woodland and grand views of Penyghent across the river.

    On reaching a wide, modern footbridge, cross and double back upstream the few strides to a gate. Now head diagonally left across the large field with Penyghent dominant ahead. Merging with Horton Beck on your left, a small footbridge on it is reached before the field corner. Across, resume on the other bank to reach a driveway at a large house. Advance briefly left along this, and approaching a cattle-grid before it becomes enclosed, bear left to a ladder-stile in the wall. Cross the small enclosure to a corner wall-stile back onto the access road. Quickest option goes left on its enclosed course, re-entering the village as suburban Chapel Lane.

Preferably, turn right on the enclosed track to a ford/ stepping-stones on Horton Beck. Just yards further is a junction of such ways alongside barns, where go left. Quickly leave by a wall-stile on the left, bearing right across the field to merge with the beck again. Through a wall-stile ahead, resume with the beck the short way to a gate/stile onto a section of old road at the village entrance. Go left onto the main road, crossing the bridge to turn right on a side road. With the beck on your right, pass a churchyard gate to shortly approach a farm. Keep left through the yard and on a short-lived stony, walled track, rising to join a similar track.

Ascend briefly right as far as a gate on the left on a minor brow, just before the way dips slightly. Cross the field to a wall-stile left of a gate and contour along a longer one to a prominent line of trees at Brants Gill Head. A wall-stile ahead (left of a fenced upper wooded section) admits to the vicinity of the beck head. This sizeable resurgence is the beck that sinks at Hunt Pot, high on the flank of Penyghent. In spate it is spectacular, a series of low falls over rock ledges heralding its return. Curve to the right, rising slightly on tussocky ground above it to a wall-stile at the other side. Head away across a sloping field to a gate onto another stony, walled track. This is Harber Scar Lane, which drops left back into the village to emerge alongside the Crown.

Horton church and Penyghent

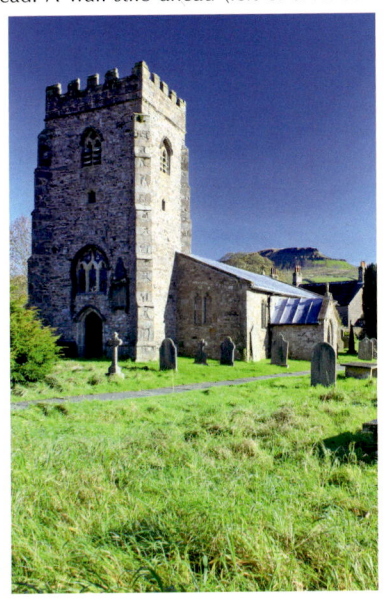

47

22 HULL POT

4¾ miles from Horton-in-Ribblesdale

Green lanes and moorland feature in a visit to a quite remarkable chasm in the lap of Penyghent

Start Village centre (SD 807726; BD24 0HE), National Park car park
Map OS Explorer OL2, Yorkshire Dales South/West
Access Open Access on Three Peaks path

For a note on Horton see page 46. From the Penyghent Café go south 80 yards and cross to a rough lane between houses out of the village. Penyghent rises ahead, with Ingleborough and Whernside rapidly joining in behind. Rising through a gate to an early fork, go left on the walled track of Horton Scar Lane rising away. After a slight dip and a curve up above a small wood, it settles down to a long, easy-angled slant, shared with the Pennine Way. After a short absence Penyghent forms an arresting sight across the deep side valley of Horton Scar on your right. The lane improves underfoot and eases further to reach its terminus at a gate onto open moor. While the Penyghent ascent path turns right, your onward route goes left. First, however, advance straight on a broad, increasingly grassy path for a few level minutes to a spectacular (and cautious!) arrival at Hull Pot.

This magnificent chasm is roughly 300 feet long and 60 feet wide, and is seen at its best when a waterfall plunges over the northern edge: under normal conditions this will have sunk underground before reaching the hole. Resume by returning to the gate, but then turn right (away from Penyghent) up a built wallside path. This is the modern route of the Three Peaks Walk, and is fully surfaced all the way to meeting the Pennine Way again on Harber Scar Lane. On a minor brow it bears away from the wall, down to a dip then climbs to meet a collapsed wall on Whitber Hill. Go right down to a wall corner, with Ingleborough and Whernside appearing ahead: the former will dominate this return walk. The path drops away and down to a wall junction, through which it bridges Sell Gill Beck and rises gently to contour left around a large, rough pasture to drop to a kissing-gate in the wall on your right. It then drops steeply with the wall to a streamlet, passing a small pothole on the right. After a slight rise it drops again onto the broad track of Harber Scar Lane. This old Settle-Langstrothdale packhorse route is very similar to your outward leg.

Turn left on this through the gate to begin a delightful return, these early stages being largely grassy with big Ribblesdale views. The track soon drops to a gate immediately through which is Sell Gill Holes. Hard by the path are an impressive stream entrance and a dry pot: the cavern below is thought to be second only to Gaping Gill in magnitude. Resuming, simply remain on this track all the way back, later becoming fully enclosed by walls as it drops down to emerge conveniently alongside the Crown.

Hull Pot and Penyghent

23 THORNS GILL

4¾ miles from Ribblehead

A beautiful old bridge and ravine are centrepiece of a tramp through wilder, upper dale country

Start Gearstones Lodge (SD 778799; LA6 3AS), lay-by to south (a mile east of Ribblehead on B6255)
Map OS Explorer OL2, Yorkshire Dales South/West

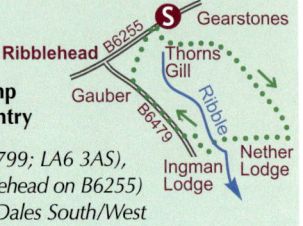

Astride a Roman road from Ingleton, Gearstones Lodge was once an inn and a shooting lodge. Head south a short way along the road, with Ingleborough's classic profile beyond Park Fell, and Penyghent further afield to the left. Ignore the first signed path and drop down to find another one just past the barn of Ribble Head House. From a hand-gate follow the left-hand wall down through further gates and by barns, then over a brow to descend to cross Thorns Gill by way of an airy packhorse bridge. This straddles a water-worn ravine of great charm, a lovely spot on the infant Ribble: note the boulders on pedestals on the opposite bank. Rise half-left, and on the brow head away by way of long crumbled walls towards a cluster of trees at the ruins of Thorns.

A short enclosed way leads to a junction in front of the main building, and here go a few strides left to a slim gate on the right into a small enclosure. From a bridle-gate opposite, head up by the wallside to the brow of Back Hools Hill, as Penyghent returns beyond drumlin-strewn moorland. Whernside is behind you, with Ingleborough hidden by Park Fell. Through a gateway drop faintly to Back Hools Barn with its partly preserved interior. From a wall-stile immediately behind it a soggy path curves around Thorns Moss to a corner gate/stile, passing above a crumbling limekiln en route. On moorland again a thinner path heads away, with Penyghent as a guide directly ahead. Bearing very gently right your thin trod slants down to cross the meandering Crutchin Gill, undulating along to negotiate some marshy terrain. Rising to a bridle-gate in a fence, Nether Lodge appears ahead. An intermittent path makes a bee-line for the farming hamlet, slanting gently down to encounter partly reedy terrain en route.

Joining the drive turn right along it, leading out through rough pasture to a bridge on the Ribble. Beyond this the access road becomes enclosed, winding up past limestone outcrops and doubling back to Ingman Lodge. With a 1667 datestone, this old house is currently extremely run down. Continue past it and up onto the B6479. Turn right for a good half-mile as far as the lone house at Gauber, in a dip on your right. En route you pass Horton/Ingleton boundary stones; a Yorkshire Wildlife Trust reserve at Ashes Pasture; and the railway cottages of Salt Lake Cottages.

At Gauber take a gate into the yard, passing a bunkbarn to reach successive small gates out into a field. Telegraph poles make a good guide as you drop steadily left to use a gate in the wall. Continue down rougher pasture to a gate in the bottom where wall and fence meet. A very faint grassy way heads away, along the base of the minor slope of Goat Close Hill to pass beneath a barn and along to a wooden bridge on a streamlet. Continue on through old walls to rise steadily to a fence-stile in front of a wooden cabin. Rise left of it to a ladder-stile in the wall above. This puts you back onto the road just south of your starting point.

*Packhorse bridge,
Thorns Gill*

24 RIBBLEHEAD VIADUCT

4¼ miles from Ribblehead

Old farmsteads linked by old ways in the shadow of Whernside and an iconic railway landmark

Start Road junction below pub (SD 765792; LA6 3AS), parking area
Map OS Explorer OL2, Yorkshire Dales South/West

Ribblehead stands where the road from Ribblesdale meets the Ingleton-Hawes road: the Station Inn has a bunkhouse. Pride of Ribblehead is 24-arch Batty Moss Viaduct, a symbol of Victorian enterprise that became the symbol of a successful campaign to prevent cynical closure of the line in the 1980s. All of the Three Peaks are well seen at various stages: mighty Whernside is in view throughout, as your walk is entirely upon its very base. Penyghent is behind you from the outset and will return near the end, while Ingleborough offers its most shapely side for much of the walk.

From the junction a hard path heads away to meet a broad track heading for the viaduct from the pub. Just before its arches the track turns to pass beneath them: instead advance straight on a firm path parallel with the railway, and after a brief pull remain on the path shadowing the line. Ignoring an early underpass, pass through a bridle-gate in a fence and Blea Moor's isolated signal box soon appears ahead. Before reaching it however, pass beneath the railway at another underpass and double back on this firm track. Ahead is Whernside, while the majestic profile of Ingleborough soon returns. The track drops down to Winterscales Beck to quickly arrive at a gate accessing Winterscales.

Pass through the old farming hamlet, crossing a stone-arched bridge to follow the access road out. Over a cattle-grid it emerges at a fork: keep right, maintaining a direct course beneath a wall with great views of the Three Peaks. It becomes enclosed at a cattle-grid to reach the farm at Ivescar. Ignoring another access road branching left, head straight on through the farm with the buildings to your right, and on to the left-hand of two gates at the end. Advance on a grassy track across a field beneath a lone house, through a gate at the end and running grandly on to a bridle-gate at an outer wall corner. The continuing grassy way narrows to a path and runs through further fields linked by bridle-gates to Broadrake Farm with its adjoining bunkhouse. Turn left down the drive, and as it turns sharp right after a cattle-grid, leave by bearing left on a grassy track down across rough pasture. At an early fork go left to a gate, the green track then crossing to ford normally dry Winterscales Beck. Across, your now fainter way curves grassily right above the dry beck to join a surfaced road.

Double back left on this farm drive until a fork just after it has bridged the beck: go right to Gunnerfleet Farm. Take the bridge on the right (the lively beck is on the surface here) and pass along the nearside of the farm buildings and out past a barn conversion: immediately both the viaduct and Penyghent are returned to view. The firm track emerges from a field to run on through the open terrain of the common back under the viaduct to finish as you began. Beneath the viaduct a monument celebrates its restoration.

Ribblehead Viaduct, with Whernside behind

25 CHAPEL-LE-DALE

4½ miles from Chapel-le-Dale

Easy walking in a fascinating area between Ingleborough and Whernside

Start Hill Inn (SD 743776; LA6 3AR), lay-bys on B6255 above pub
Map OS Explorer OL2, Yorkshire Dales South/West

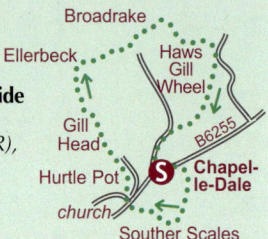

Chapel-le-Dale is a scattered community, with the Hill Inn (properly the 'Old Hill') backed spectacularly by Ingleborough. From the lay-bys, drop towards the pub but take a gate on the left, and a good track winds away past a limekiln. Through a gate a gentler green way continues, rising slightly to the next gate. Through it, abandon the Ingleborough-bound path and turn sharp right down a lesser, sunken path. At the bottom corner, the path swings left with the wall to a corner ladder-stile. Across, bear very slightly left to a broad green way dropping down parallel with the wall to a gate. Through a gateway just beyond, head away past the gaunt ruin at Souther Scales to a wall-gap left of the house. A thin path heads away, dropping to a bridle-gate below and down again through a larger pasture. Pass right of trees at the bottom to a stile in the wall below, and head away to a stile onto the B6255.

Cross over onto a narrow road to St Leonard's church. Inside is a memorial to victims from railway construction at Ribblehead - most killed by disease. Fork right here up an unsigned lane: after a cattle-grid, immersed in greenery on the right is the deep Hurtle Pot. Ignoring a branch left, the road becomes rougher to wind up to Gill Head, passing a statue with explanatory plaque. Beyond the house the road emerges onto open moorland with Whernside dominant. As it runs on to approach Ellerbeck, Ribblehead Viaduct appears over to the right. The track swings right across a streamlet to run to the farm, with Whernside now at its shapeliest. Advance to the house, and a bridle-gate to your right sends a path along a field top to avoid the farmyard. Rejoining the bridleway at another bridle-gate, a firm track heads across the field and beneath wooded limestone scars to Bruntscar. Just beyond the buildings, as the farm road turns sharp right, instead advance to a bridle-gate just ahead. A firm path crosses the next pasture to Broadrake, with adjoining bunkhouse. Turn right down the drive, and as it turns sharp right after a cattle-grid, leave by bearing left on a grassy track down across rough pasture. At an early fork go left to a gate, and the track crosses to ford normally dry Winterscales Beck. Across, your fainter way curves right above the dry beck to join a surfaced road.

Turn right and leave immediately after the cattle-grid, a path following the wall to a corner bridle-gate. With Gatekirk Cave in trees to the right, a good path follows the left-hand wall away. When it departs keep on to the far end, where the beck's brief resurgence at Haws Gill Cave just upstream quickly ends. At the end cross the dry bed to a corner bridle-gate. On your left is the deep, tree-lined bowl of Haws Gill Wheel, where the resurgent stream almost immediately sinks back below ground. From another gate just in front, cross a field as far as a small gate on the left. Here an enclosed way (natural line of the beck) runs right onto an access road. Follow it left, past Philpin farm (seasonal weekend refreshments and campsite) and onto the road just below the pub.

Chapel-le-Dale church

26 KINGSDALE

4¾ miles from Kingsdale Foot

A classic glaciated valley with outstanding limestone features

Start *Kingsdale (SD 692759; LA6 3PH), 1¾ miles on Dent road out of Thornton-in-Lonsdale: verge parking by Twisleton Lane (or on road above)* **Map** *OS Explorer OL2, Yorkshire Dales South/West* **Access** *Open Access (tiny section)*

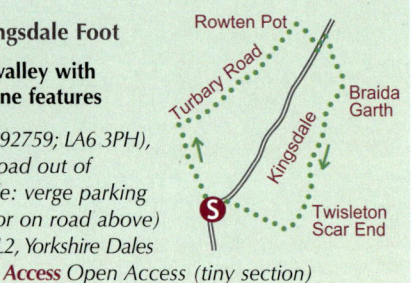

From the Twisleton Lane junction go a few yards back towards Thornton to a stile on the right. A thin trod climbs to a skyline ladder-stile, fading amid outcrops at the top: Ingleborough appears back over the valley. Initially unclear, bear left and a thin path rapidly returns to wind up through more outcrops onto a shelf with an old sheepfold to your right. Up the small gully behind, the outcrops fade as you emerge onto open pasture with Gragareth ahead and the mighty Cheese Press Stone to your left. A trod bears right over gentler ground towards a wall, rising steadily and bearing left before the wall to meet the Turbary Road at the top corner wall junction.

Turn through the gate and head off along the track. Turbary is the right to dig peat for fuel, and the 'road' was made for carts to carry it out from the Turbary Pasture. Today this splendid walkers' way along a limestone shelf offers a grand prospect of Whernside, and is a springboard for inspection of various caves and holes. Within two minutes Kail Pot is 25 yards off-track in a hollow: this deep drop is the only one safely fenced. Through a gate ahead, a parallel wall shadows you to the next gate, shortly after which you reach the dry bed of a streamlet. 150 yards left is Swinsto Hole, its unassuming entrance to an important cave system just to the right. Slant back to Turbary Pot, a distinctive hole by the track.

Beyond another gate you quickly reach the gaping chasm of Rowten Pot, a visual feast. Draped in vegetation, it drops some

350ft/106m: adjacent is a less obvious, sinister hole. Across the path is the collapsed roof of Rowten Cave, its entrance 100 yards up the moor. Don't use the gate behind, but make brief use of Open Access to turn down the wallside. Dropping by low scars, towards the bottom veer away from the wall to a gate onto the road. A few minutes to the left, a stile on the right accesses a footbridge on Kingsdale Beck's stony bed: this normally subterranean stream re-surfaces at Keld Head downstream. Heading for Braida Garth Farm, bear left to find a wall-stile on a knoll. Head away to join a firm track past the nearest barn onto the drive. Go left to the house and take a small gate on the right. Cross a small enclosure to a stile into a field beneath Braida Garth Wood, and cross to a stile/gate ahead. Continue to a stile beneath the wood end, with a ruinous limekiln and the start of a limestone scar above.

A grassy tractor track slants up through reeds to a facing stile beneath a higher bridle-gate. Head away above a wall, encountering damp, reedy terrain. Shortly after a fence takes over the going improves, and approaching denser reeds, the path bears left across rough pasture to rise to a ladder-stile in a wall ahead. Head away, rising gently near a fence through the saddle ahead. After stiles in successive walls a superior green track is joined to drop to the cart track of Twisleton Lane. Double back right, becoming enclosed to run via a footbridge on Kingsdale Beck back to the start.

Rowten Pot, looking to Whernside

27 WATERFALLS WALK

4¼ miles from Ingleton

A classic walk visiting a series of waterfalls in twin wooded gorges

Start *Village centre (SD 693733; LA6 3ET), Falls car park*
Map *OS Explorer OL2, Yorkshire Dales South/West*
Access *Much of the walk is on private land with an entry fee*

Ingleton is at the heart of Yorkshire's limestone country, an ideal base for exploring the fells, scars, caves and valleys. The centre is dominated by a railway viaduct and St Mary's church, and has pubs, cafes, shops and a youth hostel. The Waterfalls Trail has attracted visitors for well over a century, and can be worth savouring in the winter months when free of crowds. The paths are well maintained, but care is needed when wet leaves carpet the ground or in wintry conditions. Also be aware that for a low-level walk, there is substantial 'up and down' work. The two valleys explored are beautifully wooded with fascinating geological features, with the Craven Faults much in evidence.

At the car park entrance are a café, WC and a surviving section of rail viaduct on an old quarry branch. From the car park the path heads into the valley of the Twiss, passing tall cliffs on the other bank and a money tree with its own entourage. The river is crossed at Manor Bridge above Swilla Glen, just after which is a viewpoint for Pecca Falls. This is quickly followed by crossing Pecca Bridge to stand beneath the falls, a string of five that are revealed during a steep pull past distinctive Hollybush Spout. A bridle-gate into open country leads past an old refreshment hut to quickly reach the walk's highlight at Thornton Force. This massive plunge of water in a colourful setting is emphatically a place to halt.

Above it the path climbs steeply onto the glacial moraine of Raven Ray, with views left to Gragareth high above limestone scars.

A bridge takes you over the beck and up to a kissing-gate onto unsurfaced Twisleton Lane. Turn right, through a gate where an ice cream van often stands, then on beneath limestone flanks to another gate. Now surfaced, it drops the short way to Twisleton Hall, with possible refreshments. Here bear left on a track above the buildings to a stile at the end. A good path crosses the field and down to a gate onto a back road, with magnificent views to Ingleborough.

Cross straight over down the short drive to Beezleys, passing left of the buildings with WC and seasonal/weekend refreshments. With the Falls holiday park ahead, the path drops left into trees to reveal Beezley Falls. Now follow the River Doe downstream, with countless ups and downs onto viewpoint knolls. Features along the way include the pairing of Rival Falls in a gorge-like setting, then a dramatic viewing platform straddling the Baxenghyll Gorge. The lovely Snow Falls precede arrival at a bridge over the river, and the path heads away into a quarried area. A level walk runs for some time high above a steep wooded bank to emerge via a kissing-gate onto Storrs Common. The path runs on by old quarry remains, this final section enjoying an interesting prospect of tilted rock strata in Meal Bank Quarry across the beck. At the end a road-end is met to lead along to the village, joining the main street before dropping steeply down past the church to finish.

Thornton Force

28 NEWBY MOSS

4½ miles from Newby

A gentle climb to inviting moorland to discover potholes and pavements in Ingleborough's shadow

Start *Village centre (SD 728700; LA2 8HR), roadside parking*
Map *OS Explorer OL2, Yorkshire Dales South/West*
Access *Open Access, see page 4*

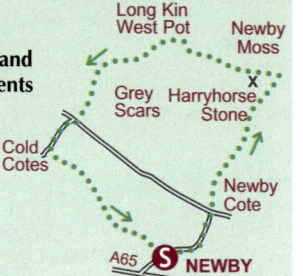

Newby is an attractive village around extensive greens, with a café on the nearby A65. Leave by the road at the top end of the green, passing Town Head Farmhouse with its 1720 datestone and sundial. The road climbs steeply to a junction with the Old Road at the hamlet of Newby Cote. Cross to the access road opposite, keeping left of several interesting buildings to rise as a walled way past an old quarry to a stile/gate onto the grassy moorland under Newby Moss. As the ascending track bears off right, remain near the wall to its top corner, noting a limekiln just over it. Behind you are big views across the Wenning Valley to the Bowland moors.

A path rises half-left to quickly cross a broader green way beneath a grassed over quarry. Keep straight up its left side and a super little path remains underfoot for a lengthy climb. Before long Penyghent appears to the right, and on a little rise by some mixed rocks, Little Ingleborough looms above. Your way angles steadily right, contouring between low limestone scars and two minutes further levelling out at a modest line of rocks. Here turn off left across pathless grass, rising gently to a prominent characterful boulder. Just 150 yards further is the isolated, very distinctive Harryhorse Stone: Ingleborough's flat summit now appears above.

Continue directly on, marginally rising to quickly reach easier terrain at the start of limestone outcrops. Advance on lush turf, rising slightly to arrive above shallow High Trough angling up from the left. Keep on the distinct edge above a sheepfold, and a little further until just before the rocks end. Here turn sharp right, possibly on a modest trod rising very slightly towards Ingleborough for two minutes to a limestone sinkhole. This sits on the edge of a colourful cluster of potholes, with mighty Long Kin West Pot at its heart. The main shaft falls 300ft/90m: take care! Your return begins by going left with the start of a reedy, sunken way, with Grey Scars just over to the left. Acquiring a thin trod it slants down to meet a broader, descending path. This leads unfailingly down the moor, finishing as a broader way through dry reeds. Deflected by sheep pens to a gate onto an access road, drop the few yards onto the Old Road.

Go briefly right to a junction at an old West Riding sign pointing you left down a narrow lane to the hamlet of Cold Cotes. The first house on your left sports a sundial, and alongside the house after it, a gate sends an enclosed path away to end at a pair of gates. From the right one follow the wall down to a corner stile, just yards beyond which is a quality stile into a field corner. Head away with the wall on your right, quickly passing through at a gate to resume on the other side. When the wall turns off towards the end, bear gently right to a wall-stile ahead. Over a slab bridge cross to a wall-stile ahead, then bear right to one near the corner. From here an enclosed footway provides a superb finish as it runs a hedgerowed course to ultimately emerge back in Newby.

Harryhorse Stone

29 NORBER BOULDERS

4¼ miles from Clapham

Grand rambling to a famous collection of alien boulders between lovely villages

Start Village centre (SD 745692; LA2 8HH), National Park car park
Map OS Explorer OL2, Yorkshire Dales South/West

   Clapham is a beautiful village through which Clapham Beck forms the centrepiece, spanned by several attractive bridges. Centrally placed are the New Inn, village store and cafe. By the car park/WC is the Manor House with a 1705 lintel, while just up the road is the church of St James with a 15th century tower. For many decades, into the 1990s, Clapham provided the cottage home to the revered Dalesman magazine. From the car park head up the road towards the church on the south side of the beck. Bear right outside the churchyard, as an enclosed bridleway takes over to pass beneath tunnels built by the Farrar family of Ingleborough Hall to access their surrounding grounds. It rises initially steeply past woodland to a junction of Thwaite Lane and Long Lane.
   Keep straight on for a long half-mile, with Ingleborough appearing back to the left. Gently descending from its high point, a stile on the left sends a grassy path away, passing right of the marshy site of a tarn. Ahead is Robin Proctor's Scar, while around you are scattered Silurian boulders. Keep right to a wall corner, following it to a corner stile beneath the scar. In Open Country advance with the wall on your right to where it drops away. Rise left to a guidepost at a path crossroads on a shelf amid scattered boulders: you are now just beneath the Norber boulderfield.
   Turning left, a sunken path squeezes between limestone outcrops onto the easier ground on which the boulders rest. Continue up the grassy path which bears right beneath a sprawling

62

cairn to reveal a great spread of large boulders ahead - time to explore! The Norber Erratics were deposited here by a retreating glacier from Crummack Dale: many of these dark Silurian rocks perch atop white limestone pedestals that have worn more rapidly away. Back at the guidepost continue down onto a lower path tracing the wall down to a gate/stile at the bottom to leave Open Country. Descend with the wall on your right, and part way along bear left on a track to a gate/stile near the corner. Rejoining Thwaite Lane, go left a few steps to join surfaced Crummack Lane, and turn right down into Austwick. At the bottom turn right to soon reach the Gamecock Inn: for a note on Austwick see page 40.

Continue past the pub to the green outside the shop, and keep right until reaching a gate/stile on the right between houses. Accessing a field corner a grassy way slants up the field, crossing to a wall-stile and another beyond, amid strip lynchets - ancient cultivation terraces. The path rises above a small wood to maintain a simple line through the fields, the latter stages seeing old iron kissing-gates replacing the stiles. Latterly a fence accompanies you along to meet the right-angle of a farm track. The path runs a parallel course to its right, later briefly entering the edge of the farmyard, and at the end running enclosed again to the car park.

Norber Boulders

30 TROW GILL

4 miles from Clapham

The absorbing valley of Clapdale leads to an impressive limestone ravine

Start Village centre (SD 745692; LA2 8HH), National Park car park
Map OS Explorer OL2, Yorkshire Dales South/West   **Access** Opening section on private land: entry fee

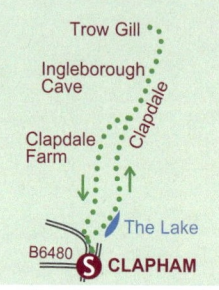

From the car park cross the road to shapely Broken Bridge and take the road right: note the waterfall plunging from the estate grounds. As the road goes left, go straight ahead as a ticket machine collects modest dues for entering the estate. A track zigzags up to the foot of an extensive, wooded lake created by the Farrers of Ingleborough Hall: botanist Reginald (1880-1920) brought alpine plants back from far-flung parts. The broad carriageway runs the length of the charming estate grounds, and climbs away from the lake, high above the beck to the 18th century Grotto. A short way beyond, you emerge into the open, upper reaches of Clapdale, and the drive shadows Clapham Beck to Ingleborough Cave. This is a showcave with guided tours. Just past it, a bridge crosses the beck within yards of its appearance at Beck Head. It last saw daylight as Fell Beck, plunging into Gaping Gill high on the moor above: a connection by cavers was only established in the 1980s.

Over the bridge pass through a gate/stile and along a dry trough between limestone scars. A corner is rounded to reveal Trow Gill, and your path passes through a gate/stile to climb into it. This former cave is now an overhanging ravine, a grand place to be. Retrace steps to Ingleborough Cave, and back along the drive. 100 yards before the woods, a stile sends a path slanting steeply up to Clapdale Farm. Turn left through a gate/stile into its yard, then away on its access road through the fields. It becomes enclosed then surfaced to drop onto a road in the village: go left to finish.